ISON SPRINGS ELEMENTARY
MEDIA CENTER

America, My Country
Explorers

Juan Ponce de León

By Moira Rose Donohue

Clarke C. Scott, M.A.
Content Consultant

Your State • Your Standards • Your Grade Level

Dear Educators, Librarians and Parents . . .

Thank you for choosing this *"America, My Country"* book! We have designed this series to support state Departments of Educations' Common Core Standards for curriculum studies AND leveled informational text. Each book in the series has been written at grade level as measured by the ATOS Readability Formula for Books (Accelerated Reader), the Lexile Framework for Reading, and the Fountas & Pinnell Benchmark Assessment System for Guided Reading. Images, captions, and other design and critical thinking elements provide supportive visual messaging and learning activities to enhance text comprehension. Glossary and Word Index sections introduce key new words and help young readers develop skills in locating and combining information. We wish you all success in using this *"America, My Country"* series to meet your student or child's learning needs.

Jill Ward, President

Publisher
State Standards Publishing, LLC
1788 Quail Hollow
Hamilton, GA 31811
USA
1.866.740.3056
www.statestandardspublishing.com

Cataloging-in-Publication Data
Donohue, Moira Rose.
  Juan Ponce de Leon / Moira Rose Donohue.
    p. cm. -- (America, my country explorers)
  Includes index.
  ISBN 978-1-93881-306-1 (lib. bdg.)
  ISBN 978-1-93881-310-8 (pbk.)
  1. Ponce de Leon, Juan, 1460?–1521--Juvenile literature. 2. Explorers--America--Biography-- Juvenile literature. 3. Explorers--Spain--Biography-- Juvenile literature. I. Title.
  972.9/02/092--dc23
  [B]

2013934118

Copyright ©2013 by State Standards Publishing, LLC. All rights reserved. No part of this book may be reproduced, stored, or transmitted in any form or by any means without prior written permission from the publisher. Printed in the United States of America, North Mankato, Minnesota, April 2013, 121312.

About the Author
Moira Rose Donohue has a Bachelor of Arts degree in political science from Mississippi University for Women and a Juris Doctorate degree from Santa Clara University School of Law. She was a banking legislative lawyer for 20 years before she began writing for children. Moira is a published author of numerous poems, plays, and articles, as well as two picture books. She loves dogs and tap dancing, and lives in northern Virginia with her family.

About the Content Consultant
Clarke C. Scott holds degrees from Central Michigan University and has 33 years of experience as a classroom teacher, building principal and system-wide administrator. Clarke most recently served as Director of Middle School Education and Lead Director for History with Pittsylvania County Schools in Virginia. He enjoys hiking, kayaking, caving, and exploring Virginia's and our nation's history. He shares his adventures both above and underground with his wife, Joyce, and family.

1 2 3 4 5 – CG – 17 16 15 14 13

Table of Contents

Knight in Shining Armor 5

Soldier, Sailor 7

Hispaniola 9

Sweet Roots and Riches 11

Royal Governor 13

Flower Power 15

Strong Currents 17

More War 19

Magical Waters 21

Glossary 22

Sound It Out! 22

Word Index 23

Explore With Bagster 24

Hi, I'm Bagster! Let's learn about Explorers.

Juan took care of the knight's armor, like this page.

Juan Ponce was born in Spain in an area called León.

Time Line

1460–1474 Born

4

Knight in Shining Armor

Juan Ponce was born in Europe in the country of Spain. He lived in the town of Santervás de Campos in an area called León. No one knows his exact birthday. Records back then were not complete. But we know Juan was born sometime between 1460 and 1474. And we know he was from a **noble**, or very important, family. Nobles added the name of the town they were from to their family names. That's why Juan was called Juan Ponce de León.

Even though Juan was a noble, his family wasn't rich. Growing up, Juan worked as a page to a knight. He had to shine the armor that the knight wore in battle! Because Juan did a good job, he got a better job and became the knight's squire. A squire takes care of the knight's swords and other weapons.

Juan sailed with Christopher Columbus on his second journey.

It's a Fact! Europeans called the Americas the New World.

Juan helped drive the Moors out of Spain in battles like this.

Time Line

1460–1474 Born

1493 Sails to New World

Soldier, Sailor

Juan learned to read and write, like children from other noble families. The knight Juan served taught him to ride a horse and to fight. The knight and Juan even went into battle against the Moors. The Moors were people from northern Africa who had **conquered** Spain. They had taken control of the country. Juan fought in the Spanish army to win Spain back. He helped drive the Moors out of Spain.

When the war ended, Juan stayed in the army. After a year, he wanted something more. He wanted to find riches and make his fortune. Juan sailed with Christopher Columbus on his second journey. Columbus was an **explorer** looking for new discoveries. He had already found the Americas across the Atlantic Ocean. Europeans called this land the **New World**. In 1493, Columbus reached the island of Hispaniola in the Caribbean Sea. Juan had landed in the Americas.

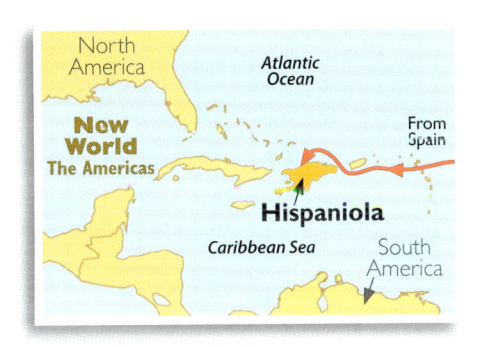

Juan lived on the island of Hispaniola.

Indians from the Taíno tribe lived on Hispaniola and other islands nearby.

Time Line

1460–1474 Born

1493 Sails to New World

8

Hispaniola

Many explorers found gold and spices and returned to their homes in Europe. Historians don't know much about what Juan did. Most think that by 1502, Juan was married and living on Hispaniola. Indians from the Taíno tribe also lived on Hispaniola and other islands nearby. The Spaniards didn't know it, but they brought sicknesses to the New World. These sicknesses killed thousands of Indians. The Spaniards also used the Indians as slaves.

The Indians became angry. They fought back. But the Spanish were strong fighters, and they had guns. Juan was in charge of the Spanish army on Hispaniola. Remember that the Moors had conquered Spain? In 1504, Juan conquered the Taínos.

It's a Fact!
Today Hispaniola is made up of the countries of Haiti and the Dominican Republic.

Hispaniola

Today Puerto Rico is governed by the United States.

King Ferdinand heard that Juan had found gold on Puerto Rico.

Time Line

10 | 1460–1474 Born | 1493 Sails to New World | 1509 Becomes royal governor

Sweet Roots and Riches

The Spanish government gave Juan land on Hispaniola to thank him for fighting the Taínos. He was also put in charge of part of the island. Juan set up a farm. He grew cassava, a root plant like a potato. Cassava was used to make sweet bread. The sweet bread didn't rot, or turn bad, as fast as regular bread. It lasted much longer on the journey home.

Juan heard about gold on the nearby island of Borinquén. Today we call this island Puerto Rico, which means "rich port." Juan sailed to Puerto Rico. He found gold! Ferdinand, the king of Spain, heard about Juan's discovery. He told Juan to search for more gold for Spain. Juan started a settlement on Puerto Rico called Caparra. In 1509, the king named Juan the first royal governor, or leader, of the island.

It's a Fact!

Today we eat cassava in tapioca pudding cups from the grocery store.

Christopher Columbus's son, Diego, did not want Juan to be in charge of Puerto Rico.

The Spaniards forced the Indians to farm and mine gold for them.

Time Line

1460-1474 Born

1493 Sails to New World

1509 Becomes royal governor

Royal Governor

As royal governor of Puerto Rico, Juan built a big stone house for his family. He had three daughters and one son. He grew sugar cane and a type of corn called maize. He grew cassava, too. He also mined gold. Juan became very rich. At first, the Taíno Indians on Puerto Rico were friendly. But soon the Spaniards forced the Indians to farm and mine gold for them. Many Indians refused. Sadly, the Spaniards killed many of them.

Christopher Columbus's son, Diego, did not want Juan to be in charge of Puerto Rico. Diego claimed that his father, Christopher, owned the island. Diego thought that he should choose the governor. And he did. Juan did not agree. Neither did King Ferdinand. The king was on Juan's side. But Diego wouldn't give up. He took the king to court! In 1511 or 1512, the judge agreed with Diego. Juan had to leave his job.

How did the Spaniards affect life on the island?

Juan landed south of St. Augustine, Florida.

Juan called the land La Florida.

Time Line

14

1460–1474 Born

1493 Sails to New World

1509 Becomes royal governor

1513 Claims Florida

Flower Power

In Juan's day, some people told tales about magical waters in the New World. Juan may not have believed in these tales of a "Fountain of Youth." But he did want riches and more land. So he asked King Ferdinand for permission to explore the island of Bimini in the present-day Bahama Islands. The king agreed.

In 1513, Juan sailed three ships to look for Bimini. But he didn't find it. Instead, he landed in present-day Florida, near today's St. Augustine. It was Easter time, a Christian holiday. Many spring flowers were growing. Easter was called The Feast of Flowers in Spanish. So Juan called the land La Florida, which means "flowery land." He claimed the land for Spain. But there were no people around. There were no riches. And it wasn't even an island.

It's a Fact!

Florida became the 27th state in 1845. Today St. Augustine is the oldest permanent Europen city in America.

North America (United States)
Gulf Stream
Spain
Europe
Asia
Atlantic Ocean
Africa
Equator
South America
North West East South

Which people might benefit from Juan's discovery of the Gulf Stream?

MY STATE

Juan made a very big discovery—the Gulf Stream.

Time Line

16

1460–1474	1493	1509	1513	1514
Born	Sails to New World	Becomes royal governor	Claims Florida	Made governor of Florida

Strong Currents

Juan continued exploring. He tried to sail south, but a strong ocean current kept pushing him north. He dropped the ship's **anchor** to hold the ship still. Juan rowed to shore in a rowboat. He didn't know it then, but he had made a very big discovery—the **Gulf Stream**. The Gulf Stream is a strong current of warm water in the ocean. It runs north along the eastern United States. Then the Gulf Stream crosses the Atlantic Ocean. Sailing in it would help ships reach Europe faster.

In 1514, Juan sailed back to Spain. King Ferdinand honored Juan by making him governor of Florida and a knight. The boy who started as a knight's page had come a long way!

It's a Fact!

The Gulf Stream warms the air in places that should be colder, like this island in England, where tropical plants grow.

Juan carried plants and animals to set up farms at the new settlement.

Time Line

- **1460–1474** Born
- **1493** Sails to New World
- **1509** Becomes royal governor
- **1513** Claims Florida
- **1514** Made governor of Florida

More War

King Ferdinand told Juan to settle Florida. But first, his country needed him to fight another tribe of Indians. The Spaniards called them Caribs. They lived on several islands in the Americas. The Caribs were attacking settlements on Puerto Rico. Juan became a fighter again. He conquered the Caribs. Juan returned to Spain once more in 1516, when King Ferdinand died. Then he went back to Puerto Rico. Now, at last, he could sail to Florida.

In 1521, Juan set sail with two ships and about 200 Spanish settlers. He also took horses, sheep, pigs, and other animals. The ship carried plants and seeds to set up farms at the new settlement. Juan sailed to the west coast of Florida. He began to build a fort to protect the colony.

Juan was wounded in his leg by an arrow.

Time Line

20 | 1460–1474 Born | 1493 Sails to New World | 1509 Becomes royal governor | 1513 Claims Florida | 1514 Made governor of Florida | 1521 Dies

Magical Waters

Another Indian tribe, the Calusas, were angry about the Spanish settlement on their land. They attacked the fort. The Calusas were strong fighters. They had weapons made from shells. Juan was wounded in his leg by an arrow. He sailed to the nearby island of Cuba to get help. But it was too late. The wound got **infected** and Juan became sick. Juan died in Cuba in July 1521. He was buried in Puerto Rico.

Juan Ponce de León conquered or destroyed many Indian tribes during his lifetime. But he explored new places. He started the first European settlement in Puerto Rico. He claimed new lands for Spain. And he found magical waters after all—the "magical waters" of the Gulf Stream.

Glossary

anchor – A heavy weight that is thrown overboard to keep a ship in place in water.

conquer – To take control of something by force.

explorer – A person who travels seeking new discoveries.

Gulf Stream – A strong, warm ocean current that moves north along the coast of Florida and then turns northeast across the Atlantic Ocean.

infected – Filled with sickness caused by germs.

New World – The name Europeans called the Americas. The New World includes the continents of North America and South America.

noble – A person who is important or has a high rank or title, like royalty.

Sound It Out!

Bimini: **bi-mih-nee**
Borinquén: **bor-rink-kin**
Calusa: **kah-loos-uh**
Caparra: **kah-par-uh**
Carribbean: **care-ih-bee-uhn**
Caribs: **care-ibz**
cassava: **kuh-sah-vah**
Diego: **dee-a-go**
Hispaniola: **his-span-yoh-luh**

Juan Ponce de León:
   wahn pahntz duh lee-ahn
    or
   pawn-say day lay-own
León: **lay-own**
maize: **mayz**
Santervás de Campos:
   san-tehr-vahs day camp-ohs
Taíno: **tie-noh**

Say these words like a pro!

Word Index

America, 7
anchor, 17
army, 7, 9
Atlantic Ocean, 7, 17
battle, 5, 7
Caribbean Sea, 7
cassava, 11, 13
claimed, 13, 15, 21
colony, 19
Columbus, Christopher, 7, 13
conquered, 7, 9, 21
country, 5, 7, 19
Diego, 13
discoveries, discovery, 7, 11, 17
Europe, Europeans, 5, 7, 9, 17, 21
explore, exploring, 7, 9, 15, 17, 21

farm, 11, 13, 19
fight, fought, 7, 9, 11, 19, 21
find, found, 7, 9, 11, 15
first, 11, 19, 21
Florida, 15, 17, 19
Fountain of Youth, 15
gold, 9, 11, 13
governor, 11, 13, 17
Gulf Stream, 17, 21
Hispaniola, 7, 19
Indians, 9, 13, 19, 21
infected, 21
island, 7, 11, 15, 21
journey, 7, 11
king, 11, 13, 15, 17, 19
knight, 5, 7, 17
land, landed, 7, 11, 15, 17, 21
magical waters, 15, 21

Moors, 7, 9
new, 19, 21
New World, 7, 9, 15
Puerto Rico, 11, 13, 19, 21
rich, riches, 5, 7, 11, 13, 15
sailed, sailing, 7, 15, 17, 19, 21
sailor, 7
settlement, 11, 19, 21
ship, 15, 17, 19
sick, sicknesses, 9, 21
St. Augustine, 15
Taíno, 9, 11, 13
United States, 17
war, 7
weapons, 5, 21

Editorial Credits

Designer: Michael Sellner, Corporate Graphics, North Mankato, Minnesota
Consultant/Marketing Design: Alison Hagler, Basset and Becker Advertising, Columbus, Georgia

Image Credits — *All images © copyright contributor below unless otherwise specified. Maps: Edward Grajeda/iStockphoto unless otherwise specified.*

Cover – "Discovering America: Juan Ponce de Leon" by Hermann Trappman, Neily Trappman Studio, Gulfport, FL. **4/5** – Ponce de Leon & Page: North Wind Picture Archives. **6/7** – War: "Battle of Higueruela 1431," by Fabrizio Castello, et al/Ian Pitchford/Wikipedia; Landing: Ivy Close Images/Alamy. **8/9** – Tainos – "Landing of Columbus"/FineArtAmerica; Hispaniola: Michael Dwyer/Alamy. **10/11** – Ferdinand: Mary Evans Picture Library/Alamy; Tapioca: HeikeRau/iStockphoto. **12/13** – Slaves: North Wind Picture Archives; Diego: Zaya Publishing/Wikipedia. **14/15** – Ponce Landing: "Discovering America: Juan Ponce de Leon" by Hermann Trappman, Neily Trappman Studio, Gulfport, FL; St. Augustine: ChoiceGraphix/iStockphoto. **16/17** – Map: John Woodcock/iStockphoto; Tresco: Stephen Rees/Shutterstock. **18/19** – Animals: "Noah's Ark," by Boyd E. Smith. **20/21** – Spaniards: North Wind Picture Archives. **24** – Globe: Globe: Alfonso de Tomas/Shutterstock.

Explore With Bagster

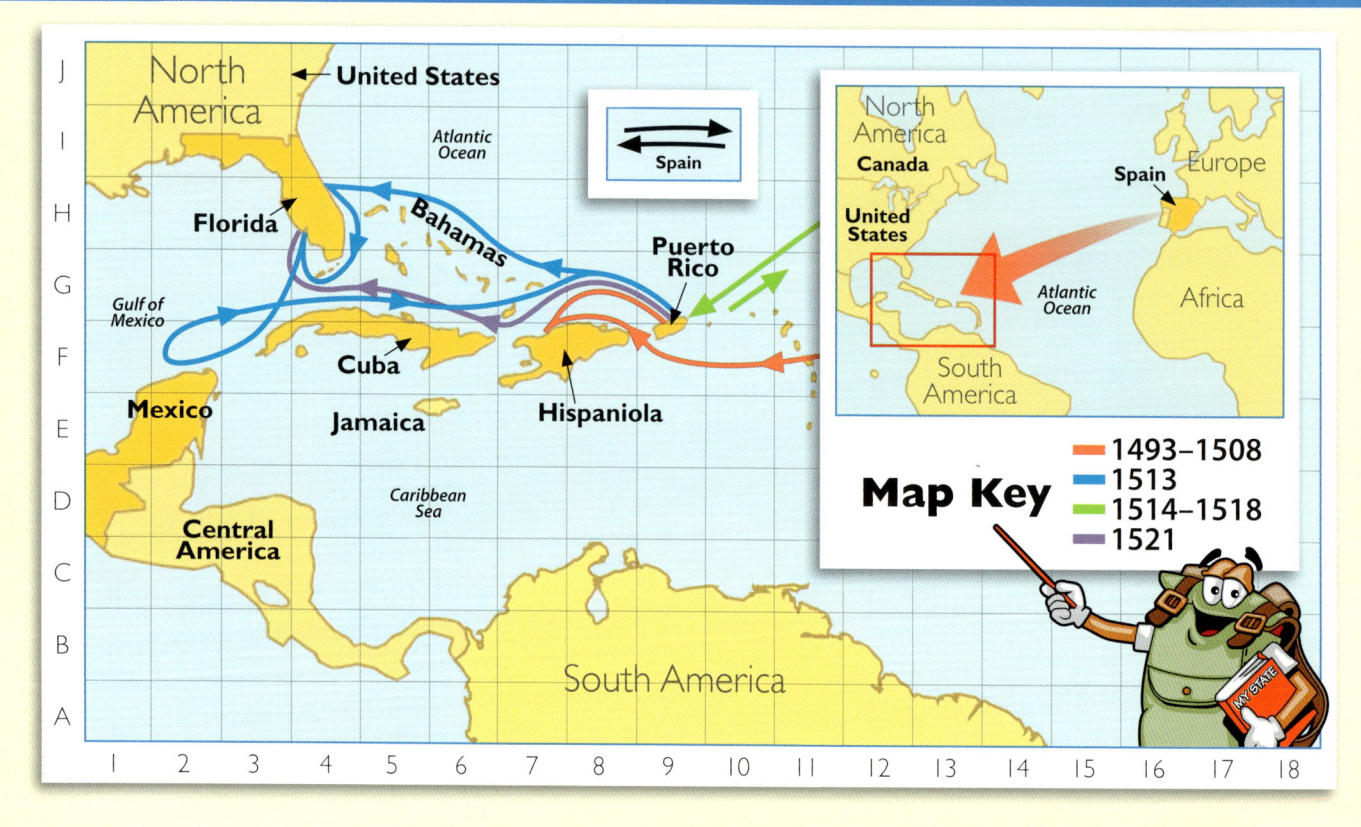

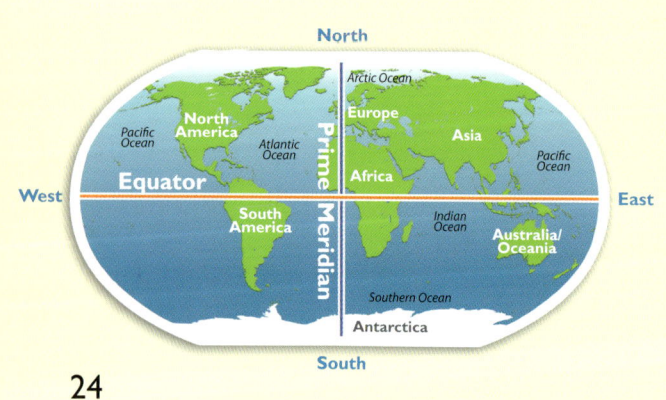

Map Key
- 1493–1508
- 1513
- 1514–1518
- 1521

Words You Should Know!

continent – One of the great divisions of land on the earth. The seven continents are: Africa, Antarctica, Asia, Australia/Oceania, Europe, North America, and South America.

equator – An imaginary line around the center of the earth that divides the Northern Hemisphere from the Southern Hemisphere.

hemisphere – Half of a sphere (the globe) created by the equator or the prime meridian. The four hemispheres are: Northern, Southern, Western, and Eastern.

ocean – A vast body of salt water. The five oceans are: Arctic, Atlantic, Indian, Pacific, and Southern.

prime meridian – An imaginary line around the center of the earth that divides the Western Hemisphere from the Eastern Hemisphere.